# nena

by Noemi

Nena
© 2019 by Noemi
Cover design by Noemi

All rights reserved. No part of this publication may be reproduced, stored in a retrieval system or transmitted, in any form or by any means, electronic, mechanical, photocopying, recording or otherwise, without permission in writing from the author.

ISBN PAPERBACK: 9781999102005
Imprint: Independently published

For information regarding permission or distribution, contact: contact@noemiii.com
Find out more about the author and upcoming books online at www.noemiii.com or @noemiii.poetry

# nena

(Spanish.) *noun.* Variation of the word *niña* meaning girl, little girl, or young female. Used to express affection or endearment.

# Contents

| | |
|---|---|
| AGE OF HEARTS ......... 10 | A THOUSAND .......... 35 |
| ELECTRIC ..................... 11 | COAX ........................ 36 |
| FAMILY ........................ 12 | THE GODDESS .......... 37 |
| REMINDER ................... 13 | OCEAN ...................... 38 |
| TO RECEIVE AND NOT DISMISS ................ 14 | STAGNANCY ............. 39 |
| | MELT ........................ 40 |
| A HUNDRED ME'S ....... 15 | SOUL TRUTH ............. 41 |
| SELF-MEDITATIONS .... 16 | MAGIC ...................... 42 |
| DEEPER WATERS ......... 17 | UNDERGROUND CATHEDRALS ......... 43 |
| FREEDOM .................... 18 | |
| PUBLIC TRANSIT ......... 19 | DON'T LIE ................. 44 |
| ANNA .......................... 20 | SELF-CARE ................ 45 |
| SMOOTH LOVE ............ 21 | COIN ......................... 46 |
| BY DEFAULT ................ 22 | MASCULINITY ............ 47 |
| AN ETERNAL SUMMER . 23 | TIMING ..................... 48 |
| FRAGILE ...................... 24 | HONEY GLAZED ......... 49 |
| VERANO ...................... 25 | AFTERNOON SKIES .... 50 |
| CONFESSIONS ............. 26 | ON MEANING ............ 51 |
| OVERFLOW ................. 27 | PAPÁ ......................... 52 |
| PERFECTION ............... 28 | PERFECT ALIGNMENTS . 53 |
| INSIDE MY HEAD ......... 29 | GUILT TRIP ................ 54 |
| BE NICE ...................... 30 | ANCESTRY ................. 55 |
| BREADCRUMBS ........... 31 | SPACE ....................... 56 |
| CAPACITY & ACTION ... 32 | COMPLICATED ........... 57 |
| THE SCULPTOR ............ 33 | THE LAST DAY ........... 58 |
| SHIT I MUST LEARN ..... 34 | LESSON PLAN ............ 59 |

| | |
|---|---|
| LEGITIMACY ......................... 60 | MIX AND SWALLOW .......... 84 |
| LIGHTER BEAUTIES ........... 61 | HEAVY HEART .................... 85 |
| NEW THINGS ........................ 62 | SOUL GARDENING.............. 86 |
| RETHINKINGS ..................... 63 | HEAT ...................................... 87 |
| 1 A.M. ..................................... 64 | VENUS ................................... 88 |
| LIT .......................................... 65 | EXPECTATIONS ................... 89 |
| POINT A IS U........................ 66 | VIDA....................................... 90 |
| STRANGER............................ 67 | CAREER ................................ 91 |
| EGO ........................................ 68 | PRIDE .................................... 92 |
| KINTSUGI.............................. 69 | LAURELS............................... 93 |
| LABOR OF LOVE ................. 70 | OBLIGATIONS ..................... 94 |
| BLUR ...................................... 71 | EMOTIONAL LABOR .......... 95 |
| UNRAVELLINGS .................. 72 | ONWARDS ............................ 96 |
| PSA ......................................... 73 | CREATION ............................ 97 |
| MULTIVERSE ....................... 74 | WARMTH ............................... 98 |
| ON PEOPLE ........................... 75 | MIND...................................... 99 |
| ON HEALING ........................ 76 | TULIPS ................................. 100 |
| SMITTEN ............................... 77 | SAFE IN SMALL DOSES.... 101 |
| LIFE PATHS........................... 78 | PINK SKIES ......................... 102 |
| DESTINY FLAWS ................. 79 | TORN.................................... 103 |
| GROWING PAINS ................. 80 | FEAR .................................... 104 |
| THE GOOD ............................ 81 | HOBBIES ............................. 105 |
| HONEY & APPLES ............... 82 | THE SCALE ......................... 106 |
| REAL WORK ......................... 83 | A KIND OF HAPPINESS .... 107 |

# AGE OF HEARTS

I now speak from the heart as much as I can. I am honest at the expense of seeming to care too much. Those who resonate with this only feed me more. Those who do not only starve themselves.

# ELECTRIC

I thought, reluctantly, that life was sorted. But sometimes change comes in the form of a person—and how frightening is that? That person walks by and it just fucking clicks. The air becomes electric. They make you feel so uncomfortable because all these possibilities are presented to you, and for the first time in a really long time, you are reminded of your duty to define yourself completely by your own accord. You are your own person, did you forget that?

# FAMILY

It blows my mind how some people could be born so broken, and others so whole. I cannot relate to paternal hatred, divorced parents, and familial silences. Some have never felt welcomed by the very forces that willed them into existence. I cannot imagine the pain—only what is so badly deserved. But it's real, it's out there, please believe me.

# REMINDER

You are responsible for your own happiness.
This is your source of power.

*NENA*

# TO RECEIVE AND NOT DISMISS

Let us teach this to all young girls: do not mistake insecurity for humility. The artificial instinct to devalue ourselves out of politeness must go. Let us yearn for women who know where they come from, but also what they are capable of. Let us untangle ourselves and learn to receive and not dismiss. Insecurity is a form of deprivation, both for yourself and those around you. Take the admiration and let it melt on your tongue; savor it. A humble soul is one that is always grateful but never wasteful, so prove that whatever is given to you—it be a compliment, an opportunity—deserves to be placed, ever so lightly, on your shoulders. Unlike the ego, all that is touched by self-worth will only bloom.

# A HUNDRED ME'S

it is not that I dislike myself
but I wish there were a hundred of me
to live all the lives that pull me
in all directions at once.

# SELF-MEDITATIONS

if you talked less about yourself
you'd know yourself better
do you see the irony in this?

# DEEPER WATERS

I've been in a strange space lately
my mind is deepening, cracking
for what's to come
something is being brewed
beneath the surface—
I feel it
the air is heavy
I am prepared.

# FREEDOM

Only time will make us realize how lucky we are to have had moments like these. Freedom is to live in both bliss and uncertainty at the same time.

## PUBLIC TRANSIT

for those girls on the bus
who, wedged between seas
of earphones and finger swiping
rest books on their laps,
dissolve into their own thoughts,
or write poems like this one.
staring, straight.
you are fermenting a quiet revolution.
I see you. I see your bright eyes.

# ANNA

the greatest lesson you taught me
with your hurricane eyes
was how much power lies
in simply holding the other's gaze.

# SMOOTH LOVE

Ice-cold March came and somehow managed to melt us. Four hours turned into seven. And then ten. And then twelve. We sat on a bench overlooking the water, talking until it got too dark to even see it. We then looked up at the stars instead. Better late than never, damn, how true that saying is. "Come with me, there's a place that always calms me down", you had told me. Looking back I should have known—that place was next to me.

# BY DEFAULT

few things delight me as when a cloudy sky
timidly breaks into blue:
a clear day may not always be in plain sight,
but it exists without fail, underneath.
beneath the hues of grey
your day, by default, is always a good one.

# AN ETERNAL SUMMER

the sweetness drips
from your smile
like peach nectar.
I could live off it, an eternal summer.

# FRAGILE

I'm not telling you to lighten up. I'm telling you to be reminded, that the mind is equal parts strong and fragile. That it will absorb whatever you give it. The soul spends your whole lifetime teaching you the lessons it knew since birth.

# VERANO

My adolescence can be condensed into gold drops of Spanish sun. From June to August, we lived in what my grandmother would jokingly call the monastery. Though quiet and isolated, it gleamed with beauty. We'd coat the house with its annual layer of white paint, and go out for walks on dirt paths that stretched towards electric sunsets. My mom and I would lay flat and count shooting stars in late July. No internet, just a church, a kiosk, and one small supermarket for the whole village of four hundred people. Old folks sat in rows against the walls of their houses. On Sunday mornings we'd wait for my grandmother to apply her L'Oreal lipstick so we could finally cram ourselves into two cars to drive to the next town over, past the vineyards and corn fields to get nectarines and fresh olives at the market. Our week's highlight were the friends and family who'd drop by, arriving and leaving on Mediterranean time. In the afternoon came the quiet lull of siesta hour, when we'd sneak around to see what the others were up to. Solitude rested amongst the swaying fruit trees and clouds hung so low you could almost touch them. Almost.

*NENA*

# CONFESSIONS

In the most unexpected moments, his guard would slip. He'd reveal a moral compass so sharp and so earnest that it surprised me everytime. I fell in love. I watched him and thought to myself, "this kind of person can only be built with a lot of love or a lot of pain."

# OVERFLOW

Please remember that sometimes, people will insist on doing certain things for you purely out of love. It's their way of expressing affection—and they will want to do them regardless of how inconvenient, how unnecessary, or how annoying it might be for you. It's ok. Be patient. Let them have their moment. Let them insist on brushing your hair because they think it looks terrible, or giving you a massage when you don't need one, or picking you up when you don't have the energy for a night out. When love overflows, we run around looking for things to water. Let your loved ones do the things they cannot help but do. It helps them to water themselves, too.

# PERFECTION

Progress over perfection. Whatever you have been meaning to get to, start now. Enough waiting—nothing be perfect without existing first.

# INSIDE MY HEAD

I wish I could show you the sunniness of my mind, the bliss, how exquisitely warm it is in here. Because somehow the beautiful translates into naïve daydreams when spoken aloud. No wonder I can't explain myself well. It's far too comfortable and perfect here, inside my head.

# BE NICE

If I should be nice to others, why shouldn't I be nice to myself?

# BREADCRUMBS

Enough with the sadness. No, seriously. How much of it is justified, and how much of it are you creating for yourself? Man cannot live on bread alone, and sadness is the breadcrumb of all human emotions.

# CAPACITY & ACTION

There is a fine line between capacity and action. Of course you could do what they do—it may not take a lot of time or money or even effort to emulate their achievements. But potential pales in comparison to action. The things that materialize are the things that stay; potential is only significant when it becomes something more. Know that once you achieve something it cannot be taken away from you. Let them speak, whether they be your own bad thoughts or those of others. We all have capacity—but the action makes the difference.

# THE SCULPTOR

intellectuals
come in many forms
but this one was the purest.
he told me he was a sculptor
so the softness I found in his eyes
was probably in his brown hands too.
hearing him speak
I realized that the greatest intellectual
is also an artist.

# SHIT I MUST LEARN

Passiveness is not kindness. Kindness is not passiveness.
Passiveness is not kindness. Kindness is not passiveness.
Passiveness is not kindness. Kindness is not passiveness.

# A THOUSAND

*(sometimes I think friendships are purer than romantic love. What a beautiful thing to be loved without lust, just loyalty. And what a strange thing when it ends. But some things end only to bloom again.)*

You were in my dreams the other day. And now you come and tell me that I keep reappearing in yours. If it's true that dreams are what happens to us in other dimensions or that they are what we've experienced in a past life, I suppose we keep colliding into each other under fate's magnetism. "I would still open my heart a thousand times for you". I wrote that when I woke up that morning. In this life, in the next, in a thousand alternate dimensions—it would still be true.

# COAX

Someone recently asked me how to work through someone else's trauma and psychological hardships. "You…you just do it", I said. I didn't know how else to put it. Where there is love there is softness. Of course you can't save someone—that's not your responsibility, and that's not your power. But you can coax. You can coax the hell out of someone, and I say that almost literally. No one is born with their fears—they are learned, embodied, and naturalized over time. It coats their character and hardens them. But the best part is, you don't need to fully understand in order to support them. Yes, do the research, ask the questions, get perspective. But sometimes "I'm here for you, even if it doesn't make sense to me sometimes"…sometimes that's all that's needed. I'm not saying it's easy (hell no); I'm saying it's worth it.

# THE GODDESS

the goddess within
longs for sunkissed skin
opulent bath soaks
and an infinite library.

# OCEAN

there's a funny thing that happy people do.
you give them a drop of love,
and they give you an ocean back.

# STAGNANCY

I've learned that you can't trick yourself into believing that stability and continuance means progress. Progress is not what has always been—that's stagnancy. I fooled myself so many times believing that my relationship was going somewhere simply because it had accumulated a respectable amount of years. To move forward is to look at the future and gradually inhabit it. Please don't be afraid to think about the future. Please understand that it needs to exist if you want good things to happen. Please do not mistake stability for progress.

# MELT

I now know
how to melt the uncomfortable
to extract
the loveliest parts of myself
in the roughest of moments.

# SOUL TRUTH

I realize now I could never live any other way. I was meant to live slowly, quietly. My life will irrefutably be so typical of me—filled with art, simple days, and so much thinking. I know you always wanted something different for me, mama. But my soul always knew this, and I am remembering it now.

# MAGIC

do not be fooled—
beauty is not the true ideal
it is a mere echo of the real thing;
magic.

*NENA*

# UNDERGROUND CATHEDRALS

I like to think that my life is a beautiful one. Most of it is upheld by personal philosophies that rarely exist outside of my own head; they are tucked away like underground cathedrals, ornate and divine. I suppose I've always been attracted to ideals, to the abstract, and that is just what they are. These philosophies including the one you are reading, pull me away from the mundaneness of what is before me. To capture the things we see without sight, the things we dream about, the things we are subjective towards…that's what colors life, no? My highest goal in life is to bridge the gap between the everyday and the ideal. The temporary and the eternal. Because the most exciting, most meaningful things in life come from that collision.

# DON'T LIE
*(trigger warning)*

isn't it ironic
how the stories told by women
are not believed by men
when they've looked at a woman
at least once in their lives
and have considered writing their own
upon her body.

# SELF-CARE

The sick cannot heal the sick.

# COIN

So often, the reason something makes you happy becomes the very reason you fall out of love with it. We originally see these things as solely good, without considering what it could look like in scenarios beyond the one we are in. A person's hardworking character might be what you admired, but it is also the reason they become a workaholic. The unique way you earned your job might be the very manner by which that opportunity is passed on to someone else. Only context (i.e., what is best at that time, what you have come to prefer) determines whether you find that trait attractive. Be careful, be observant. Don't be so shocked if there comes a change in heart or circumstance—it is more familiar than you think.

# MASCULINITY

quiet masculinity
a rare sight.
a soul so clear
I see all the way down
to still, dark waters.

# TIMING

Who you long for is based entirely on who you are in that precise period of your life. You view that person as everything you've ever looked for because they align with your character, self-knowledge, your belief systems, your traumas...all of which is constantly being rewritten. This is why I don't believe in soulmates: you cannot predict what you will want or who you will be in a decade, in five years, or even one year from now. Do not expect yourself to be standing in the same place in the sand after waves crash over your feet time and time again. And *this* is why I believe in timing: it is the make or break of the universe. The heart wants what it wants. So when it pulls you, drags you, regardless of how that person might feel about you, you tell it; "if it's worth my time it'll align in the way I need it to. If I've given it a chance and it hasn't worked, it's only what I want, not what I need."

# HONEY GLAZED

all this love
like honey-glazed rose petals.

# AFTERNOON SKIES

there's that fleeting moment in the evening,
before the light changes
when the sky is at its softest.
dripping in gold
and so forgiving,
it reminds me that the world
was whatever I wanted it to be that day.

## ON MEANING

there is meaning in each single atom
that sustains this existence.
between these lines
in the crevice of each letter
find it,
it is yours to keep.

# PAPÁ

I was sniffling (read: crying) in public while we were looking at fountain pens. It was so busy, so hot in there. Salesclerks watched me uncomfortably. Under your breath you asked me what was wrong—they were the same troubles as always. And you said those magic words parents can say so well, regardless of whether or not it concerns them: "I'll take care of it. Don't worry." Oh how everything melted in that moment. It was then I was reminded of the difference between a boy and a man.

# PERFECT ALIGNMENTS

I've come to learn there are parts of ourselves that only come to light in the presence of certain people and places. We like to think that we know ourselves, and that know ourselves well. But every so often things resurface: we are rarely who we think we are. Like the layering of watercolors, soft and translucent, there comes a shift. Shapes are drawn from the hues, the arcane is revisited.

# GUILT TRIP

Do not let other people guilt you into feeling the way they do.

# ANCESTRY

Stories upon stories, laid atop the backs
of men and women.
A never-ending loop of sunsets that bleed
from one generation to the next,
their heads crowned in the dark by the same arctic stars as mine.
Something will come from this. And it will remain.
Creation is too beautiful of a thing not to do.

# SPACE

If I can't be inspired by it
Why should I give it space in my life?

# COMPLICATED

You are getting in your own way. You. Get it done, keep it moving, do not bother. If you are not your greatest ally, the smallest pebble becomes a boulder. It is not about the magnitude of your problems (it never was); just find a way to make it work. Do not second-guess yourself so much. This does not have to be so complicated.

*NENA*

# THE LAST DAY

One day it will be the last day and you won't even realize it. One day, it will be the last time you visit that place, play that game as children, or share that bed. Little do you know that the promise you made—saying "see you soon" over your shoulder—will never happen. Life as you've come to understand it will fade softly and you will be too preoccupied to notice. Life is given away in increments, to new people and moments. One day it will be the last day.

# LESSON PLAN

If it's about you, choose freedom.
Always.

# LEGITIMACY

If someone feels uncomfortable towards a person or situation, their feelings are always legitimate. Period. Feelings aren't always reality but they will always hold weight for those who feel them. If someone tells you they feel uncomfortable, raise your hands and walk away. It is not your place to tell them where their boundaries lie.

## LIGHTER BEAUTIES

the aching may be beautiful
but tiring too.
I'm done being consumed by it—
there are lighter beauties out there
to be enjoyed.

# NEW THINGS

I'm starting to think that experiencing something for the first time is really what makes it so meaningful. Nothing else. We can grow accustomed to practically anything—no matter how good or bad—but our adaptive trait is as strong as our drive for progress. The fact that it's new, different, unprecedented...*that* is what matters. And that is exactly what terrifies me.

# RETHINKINGS

It's funny how my words have been reinvented. They sound differently now. They taste differently now. Nothing stays the same, not even meaning itself. And now that these words are not meant for you, I'm starting to think that life is made of tiny threads of relevance that tie us back to our little worlds. Call it selfish but it was never about you—it was about me and those threads that no one could see—let alone understand—when I said I loved you.

# 1 A.M.

don't trust your feelings at night.
things fall apart at the end of the day
only to be rebuilt in the morning.
cry if you must
but there is a softening
a humbling
that comes with morning light.

## LIT

"Wouldn't it be beautiful if man first discovered fire though embrace?" I asked in the dark. Not given, not taught, but found and made, in the arms of another. Friction, heat, spark. Kindled souls, illumined world.

# POINT A IS U

begin with you:
that is where it must start.
always.

# STRANGER

There are only two instances in which I pray—when I hear sirens, and when I notice a stranger with a special type of kindness. There's a softness, a subtlety in their "hello". It's in their manners, their replies, the way they carry themselves. They are that streak of sunlight, that rarity that makes me want to clutch them and say "you deserve the whole world". I cannot help but give them everything I can, which is quite little. They will never know that when our encounter ends, I pray under my breath that life will protect them and give them everything they will need.

# EGO

Selfless good deeds are not real. You will always get something out of it, because there is no giving without adding. It is not about getting rid of the ego, but about working with it. It is there to protect you. Play it to your advantage.

# KINTSUGI

when things are mended after a fight
I swear on my life it's the sweetest feeling.
to share that look
that admits a beautiful kind of defeat
means gravity is restored
once again
and hearts return to orbit
around each other.
together you've burned that which doesn't serve purpose
and once again
have adjoined the cracks with gold.

# LABOR OF LOVE

Everything that is important in life requires effort.
What makes you think true love is any different?

# BLUR

I'm beginning to realize that your current and future self are not very different. That time blurs faster than you know. That who you think you are is mostly based on who you've been yesterday. There is only one you, ever-changing, Please don't trust that your future self will be any different from who you are today—whatever you will be, you already are in small measures. Recognize and amplify those aspects you wish to be defined by. In retrospect, you'll see that where you stand is not a surprise. So move quickly, move now.

# UNRAVELLINGS

My self-unravellings have led me to remember my simplicity. All of this we impose on ourselves, the harm we create, the triviality of the things we blow out of proportion…how did we lead ourselves so astray? The uncomplicated soul is the least lonely one. To return not to simple minds, but simpler hearts—that is where I wish to go.

# PSA

almost all bitterness
comes from resistance to change.

# MULTIVERSE

if the multiverse is comprised of words
and our thoughts are constellations
choose very carefully
which worlds to occupy.

# ON PEOPLE

Forget the miserable poems that are written about betrayal, heartbreak, and wretched souls. Forget the poets whose lips cannot speak about anything but betrayal. People are everything—they are the stories we live. They link us to something beyond ourselves. Do not give up on them.

# ON HEALING

your heart must grieve
as much as it must find peace.
let its landscape be carved by new fractures,
new canyons of experience.
to heal is not to get over—
it is to create something new.

# SMITTEN

I can't help it—my soul is in love with yours.

# LIFE PATHS

Sometimes I look at people as representations of paths I could have taken in life. People are inspiring with their stories, but rarely do we see them for what they truly are—a culmination of experience, decisions, and habits. It is easier to view others for what they are now rather than to consider how they got there. We are not who we are for no good reason.

# DESTINY FLAWS

There are certain mistakes that are meant to be made by certain people. Each individual has lessons that must be learned through direct experience. These lessons vary from person to person—what may be instinctive knowledge to you is a lesson to be learned firsthand by someone else. You cannot change a person's course of life learning; you can only support them and recognize that your world differs from theirs.

This is the closest thing to fate.

# GROWING PAINS

the soul will grow into this.
it's just growing pains.

# THE GOOD

The good will come. I believe in its capacity to make me happy, even if I may not know what it exactly looks like. I always know what I *think* I want, but not what I need, let alone deserve. Life knows me better than I know myself—all I can do is give it my best. Everything that happens after is magic.

# HONEY & APPLES

I think that our character gets refined over time. Some people rot like sour apples, others mellow like aged honey. What has always been there will come to its totality with old age. Time will reveal that which cannot be hidden. What will it reveal about you?

# REAL WORK

once the rage is gone,
the embers burn hard and quietly.
that is when the real work begins.

# MIX AND SWALLOW

There is nothing more feminine than a combination of
sweetness and power. It is all that I want. To be cloaked in
softness, to be both alluring and restless. It is like
swallowing the sky
the clouds
and sun.
let them reside in me,
let them leave me brimming with their potency.

# HEAVY HEART

what is this that we do:
fight, fix
break, mend
perhaps it is all, at once—
the heart gets restructured in strange ways.

# SOUL GARDENING

Everyday is a chance to create something. To me, that is the most exciting thing we are able to do as human beings. On some days it comes easily—your day begins with an already-blooming, fruitful garden. Other days your hands are in mud. And some days you just cannot do it alone. That's fine; let it come as it may. Use what you have and the rest will follow.

# HEAT

you're seeking battles everywhere you look
because you're craving that fire.
that heat it produces
charges you
is mouthwatering to you
because I think deep down inside
you hate that you can't spark
such heat within yourself
without violence.

# VENUS

vocal cords on fire
the night air is getting sweeter
like the clouds above
cherry blossom trees
blur past us
oh what an honor
to be loved by you.

# EXPECTATIONS

the sad truth is,
nothing changes
if nothing changes.

# VIDA

Life has a way of proving you wrong in all the right ways.
Stay watchful.

# CAREER

I never knew what I wanted to do for a living. I only knew what I wanted out of life—that is, to make beautiful things and to be happy. At the end of the day I believe having a heart is all that matters. Live by it and you will spend your entire life dipping your feet in worlds of splendor, lured from one fascination to the next. It might not get you to all the places, but it will get you started; talent will be gathered effortlessly because you will never be satisfied with what you have learned and explored. I truthfully cannot think of a lovelier way to experience life.

# PRIDE

I hope you learn soon enough
that apologies and pride do not mix

to be able to admit when you are wrong
and say you could have done better
is not defeat

if that is all they want
you are not the one who loses.

# LAURELS

do not rest on your laurels—
it only takes one second, one moment to destroy something
that takes a lifetime to build.

# OBLIGATIONS

We like to think that we are easy to love, but believe me; we are all much harder to love than we think. Only you are obligated to remain with yourself. Anyone who stays sees more in you than you can imagine. Cherish these people.

# EMOTIONAL LABOR

*noun.*
the act of ensuring the emotional comfort of others. Can quickly result in fulfilling problematic expectations in order to appease or pacify.

I want all girls to understand the term emotional labor. Since language shapes reality, I want all girls to have the tools they need to think in ways that help them protect themselves. I want them to realize how much of the everyday work they do is unpaid, unsolicited, and gendered. We should all strive to empathize with others and provide support, but please be careful. Emotional labor is as real as any labor. What makes it especially dangerous is that we've been told it isn't what "work" looks like. Because it is expected both in the workplace and outside of it. Because it is seen as "passive" labor. Because it is to be offered to anyone and everyone. Take note: the fact that you are not being paid for something does not devalue its worth. Understand what you are giving away.

## ONWARDS

how dare they attempt to guilt us
for leaving
for the better.

# CREATION

just as the universe ceaselessly creates
(planets, life, symphonies)
we mimic in typical human manner
(making art, memories, meaning)
because wouldn't you say
that it is when we create
that we feel the most alive?

# WARMTH

I will always say that life is worth it. That as long as we have the capacity to feel, we have everything.
That the best place to be is here, right now.
To be able to feel the warmth of the sun, have endeavors and dreams, and to not live in fear but curiosity for the unknown—that is all I need.

# MIND

There is little that can be done
When the mind thinks so.

# TULIPS

Even the most transitional phases of life deserve to be experienced well. I realized this when she kicked open the door to our small basement suite with a handful of freshly cut flowers from the backyard. It was a crumby little place with yellow paint peeling off the walls, but she still crowned it with tulips. There were small vases of flowers everywhere: in the kitchen, on the living room table, and even in the bathroom. And although they would only last a week, she knew that wasn't the point. Living well (while still within your means) should never be put on hold—anything less is merely existing.

# SAFE IN SMALL DOSES

sometimes it's healthy
not getting what you want.
remember this.

# PINK SKIES

Life could be miserable.
or it could be
exploring new cities
and going peach-picking in the summertime
it could be getting better jobs, making the best mistakes
and celebrating love.
it could be looking at pink evening skies
and creating new worlds.
It could be.

# TORN

I'm torn between a modest life and having more than I could ever need. A part of me wants the sleepy days in a quiet town, but another has a voracious appetite for possibility. And although the split gnaws at me everyday, I cannot afford to lose either of them—they are both parts of me.

# FEAR

We sat at that bench. He told me his greatest fear was that he would finish living and think it wasn't worth any of it. Goddamn. I could only laugh—it was so bizarre to me how different our thoughts were. If it wasn't worth it, ok. Why should it matter? For whatever reason, you are here now—give it a chance. None of this is meant to make any sense. Just enjoy the good, dismiss the bad. If it all comes and goes so easily, what is the harm?

# HOBBIES

So much of what we do not do is because we lack time. We could have such different lives if we simply had enough time to cultivate them. Yet we are either too reckless or too passive, and give away our counted breaths.

You could be more of yourself if you just had the time for it—how strange does that sound?

# THE SCALE

I think there are a lot of embittered people out there.
Antagonistic people who don't know how to express
themselves
without regret
without pain
because they still think
that the world is out to get them.
because they still think
that that's what gives them character.
but that isn't character—
that's merely attitude.
*character*
is honesty
it's integrity
it's self-reflexivity
it's thinking about yourself
and loving it
without hating on the world around you.
stop thinking like you are on one end of a scale
and the world on the other. The world is not driven by
misery and you should not be either.

# A KIND OF HAPPINESS

Maybe one day I'll have a house made of sunlight. A small one, with flowers hanging from the ceilings. It won't have much—no, it'll have everything. I'll sip my morning tea and look out the window and let time come and go as it pleases. I'll have my outfits, I'll go out for walks, and I won't ask for much. Maybe you'll live there too. You'll have your garden and your bees and I'll watch you, between the wisterias, while I write my things. I don't want anything else, I really truly don't. Just a bright, quiet kind of happiness

*i love you.*

www.ingramcontent.com/pod-product-compliance
Lightning Source LLC
Chambersburg PA
CBHW051657040426
42446CB00009B/1182